ry

D1278274

)

FIREFIGHTERS

Rescue and Prevention: Defending Our Nation

- Biological and Germ Warfare Protection
- Border and Immigration Control
- Counterterrorist Forces with the CIA
- The Department of Homeland Security
- The Drug Enforcement Administration
- Firefighters
- Hostage Rescue with the FBI
- The National Guard
- Police Crime Prevention
- Protecting the Nation with the U.S. Air Force
- Protecting the Nation with the U.S. Army
- Protecting the Nation with the U.S. Navy
- Rescue at Sea with the U.S. and Canadian Coast Guards
- The U.S. Transportation Security Administration
- Wilderness Rescue with the U.S. Search and Rescue Task Force

RESCUE AND PREVENTION: Defending Our Nation

FIREFIGHTERS

BRENDA RALPH LEWIS

MASON CREST PUBLISHERS
www.masoncrest.com

Mason Crest Publishers Inc.
370 Reed Road
Broomall, PA 19008
(866) MCP-BOOK (toll free)
www.masoncrest.com

First printing

1 2 3 4 5 6 7 8 9 10

Library of Congress Cataloging-in-Publication Data on file
at the Library of Congress

ISBN 1-59084-402-5

Editorial and design by
Amber Books Ltd.
Bradley's Close
74–77 White Lion Street
London N1 9PF
www.amberbooks.co.uk

Project Editor: Michael Spilling
Design: Graham Curd
Picture Research: Natasha Jones

Printed and bound in Jordan

Picture credits
Federal Emergency Management Agency (FEMA): 27, 54, 60; Mary Evans Picture Library: 10, 19, 20; Popperfoto: 6, 9, 13, 14-15, 16, 22, 24, 25, 26, 28, 29, 30, 32–33, 36, 38, 41, 42–43, 44, 47, 49, 50, 52, 55, 56, 58, 59, 61, 64, 66, 67, 69, 70, 72, 73, 74, 75, 78, 80, 83, 84–85, 86; Topham Picturepoint: 89.
Front cover: Popperfoto.

DEDICATION

This book is dedicated to those who perished in the terrorist attacks of September 11, 2001, and to all the committed individuals who continually serve to defend freedom and protect the American people.

CONTENTS

Introduction   7

Firefighting in the Past   9

Training to be a Firefighter   23

Fires in the City   37

Wildland Fires   51

Aircraft on Fire   65

Firefighting in the Future   79

Glossary   90

Chronology   92

Further Information   94

Index   96

INTRODUCTION

September 11, 2001, saw terrorism cast its lethal shadow across the globe. The deaths inflicted at the Twin Towers, at the Pentagon, and in Pennsylvania were truly an attack on the world and civilization itself. However, even as the impact echoed around the world, the forces of decency were fighting back: Americans drew inspiration from a new breed of previously unsung, everyday heroes. Amid the smoking rubble, firefighters, police officers, search-and-rescue, and other "first responders" made history. The sacrifices made that day will never be forgotten.

Out of the horror and destruction, we have fought back on every front. When the terrorists struck, their target was not just the United States, but also the values that the American people share with others all over the world who cherish freedom. Country by country, region by region, state by state, we have strengthened our public-safety efforts to make it much more difficult for terrorists.

Others have come to the forefront: from the Coast Guard to the Border Patrol, a wide range of agencies work day and night for our protection. Before the terrorist attacks of September 11, 2001, launched them into the spotlight, the courage of these guardians went largely unrecognized, although in truth, the sense of service was always honor enough for them. We can never repay the debt we owe them, but by increasing our understanding of the work they do, the *Rescue and Prevention: Defending Our Nation* books will enable us to better appreciate our brave defenders.

Steven L. Labov—CISM, MSO, CERT 3

Chief of Department, United States Search and Rescue Task Force

Left: Having been dropped into the midst of a fire from a helicopter, a "rappeler" firefighter prepares to combat a wildland fire in Arizona.

FIREFIGHTING IN THE PAST

Fire has always been important in everyday life. It provides warmth and security, but it is also dangerous and can destroy. In prehistoric times, it was used to warm caves and cook food; big fires were lit at night at the entrance to the caves so that wild animals would be frightened away. However, fires can also burn out of control, burning down entire forests, or turning houses and other buildings into smoking ashes. Fire can kill people by burning them to death or by choking them with the smoke it creates.

FIRES IN THE CITIES

The danger of fire became even greater some 6,000 years ago when people began to live in cities in and around Mesopotamia (present-day Iraq). The ancient Egyptians were well aware of this and used hand-operated wooden pumps to put out fires in the second century B.C. The problem in the ancient cities was that people lived close together: they had their own fires and cooking stoves, so a single outbreak of fire could quickly spread, destroying homes and killing people. In the towns and cities of the ancient Roman Empire, this happened all-too-often in badly built, overcrowded three- or four-story apartment blocks called **insulae**, or islands.

Left: For these children, fire hydrants provide a useful way of cooling down in New York City's hot, sticky summers. This picture was taken in Brooklyn in 1952.

In A.D. 64, the Roman Emperor Nero is said to have played his fiddle while Rome burned. In fact, he did a great deal to help Rome to recover from the fire by organizing relief and rebuilding programs.

All it took to start a fire and, often burn down the entire building, was for someone to have an accident while cooking a meal. Starting in one apartment, the blaze could spread through the insula within a few minutes and then threaten neighboring buildings. This was why there were teams of **vigiles**, or watchmen, who patrolled the streets of Roman cities. Their primary job was to deal with any sort of trouble—including fights or murders— but they were also the firefighters who dealt with blazing buildings, putting out the fires and rescuing people trapped by the flames. There were 7,000 vigiles in ancient Rome itself.

Unfortunately, the vigiles were not always successful. Certainly, they were unable to handle a really big fire, like the huge **conflagration** that destroyed two-thirds of ancient Rome in A.D. 64. It started on July 18 in the Circus Maximus, a place of public entertainment where chariot races were held, and it burned for more than a week. Ten out of Rome's 14 districts were completely destroyed, as temples, public buildings, and thousands of homes went up in flames. There were terrible scenes as Romans ran out of the city, screaming in panic.

Nero, the Roman Emperor, was not in Rome when the fire started, but 33 miles (53 km) away to the south, at Antium (modern Anzio). He seems to have done his best to help, organizing food supplies and setting up temporary homes. All the same, a rumor spread that he was the one who had set Rome alight. It was said he wanted to build himself a larger p_ and thought th_ was so ru_

A FIREMAN'S PRAYER

When I am called to duty, God

Wherever flames may rage

Give me the strength to save some life

Whatever be its age

Help me embrace a little child

Before it is too late

Or save an older person from

The horror of that fate

Enable me to be alert and

Hear the weakest shout

And quickly and efficiently

To put the fire out...

And if according to Your will

I have to lose my life

Please bless with Your protecting hand

My children and my wife

(Anonymous)

deserved to be destroyed. According to the gossips, Nero stood on the roof of his palace and "fiddled," or played, his **lyre** while Rome burned. No one knows if any of this was true, but after the fire, Nero set about rebuilding Rome as a much more splendid city, with fine buildings and a grid system of roads.

LONDON'S BURNING

Three years earlier, another city of the Roman empire—London, capital of the Roman province of Britannia—went up in flames when a rebel British queen, Boudicca, attacked the city and burned it. After this, in A.D. 63, the Romans decided to appoint vigiles to look out for fires in London. London kept its vigiles until the Romans abandoned Britannia in around A.D. 426, returning to Rome to defend it against attacks by barbarian tribes. Unfortunately, the vigiles departed with the Romans, and London had no proper fire service for another 1,250 years.

In 1212, London Bridge burned down. The consequences were severe. Not only are 12,000 people reported to have died, but London Bridge was at that time the only bridge across the Thames River, which runs through the city.

The burning of London Bridge was known as the Great Fire of London until an even greater and much more damaging fire broke out in September 1666. At that time, London still had no fire service—the capital's first fire brigade was not formed until 1680. great fire burned for over four days, and the flames burned ost of London's big buildings, including Saint Paul's Cathe- stroyed around 13,000 homes. The flames could be seen nearly 40 miles (64 km) away. The fire began in a baker's shop in Pudding Lane and spread rapidly. Before long, a huge cloud of black, choking smoke, "like the top of a burning oven," hung over the city. The king of England, Charles II, and his brother James, Duke of York, helped to fight the flames by organizing firefighting

This engine, on show at the London Bridge Exhibition in 1931, is thought to be the world's oldest surviving fire engine. As indicated on its side, the engine would have originally been stationed in Crooked Lane, London, although it was later discovered at St. Michael's Church.

These firemen, pictured in 1937,
had been driving for 12 years, having
never passed a driving test. In
remembrance of these men, the Crawley
firemen in Sussex, England, still display an "L" on
their engines, the British symbol indicating that the driver is "learning."

teams and pulling down buildings to make **firebreaks**. But the flames leapt across the firebreaks, and John Evelyn, a famous English diarist, described what followed:

"There was nothing heard or seen but crying out and lamentation, running about like distracted creatures as [the fire] burned both in breadth and length, leaping from house to house and street to street; for the heat had even ignited the air, and the fire devoured houses, furniture, and everything."

It took a long time for London to recover from this disaster. Many Londoners were unable to return to the city to live until 1672, six years later.

BENJAMIN FRANKLIN AND THE LIGHTNING ROD

In colonial America, Boston got its first fire brigade in the same year as London—1680. The firefighters were paid to put out fires, but in 1735, Benjamin Franklin had a different idea. He formed the first volunteer fire department in Philadelphia, believing that putting out fires should be a public duty.

Franklin was also worried by the thatched straw roofs most Americans put on their houses. It was far too easy for sparks or embers from chimneys to set the roofs on fire. Another problem was lightning strikes that hit the roofs during thunderstorms and set them ablaze. To stop

Even today, people still use buckets of water to fight fires. This fireman can be seen silhouetted against a burning hot sun in Bulgaria. A heat wave in July 2000 triggered many fires throughout the country, especially in woodland areas.

this from happening, Benjamin Franklin invented the lightning rod. This makes the lightning discharge into the ground and prevents it from setting houses on fire.

THE BUCKET BRIGADES

At first, there were no fire engines that could pump out water to extinguish the flames. Instead, there were "bucket brigades"—long lines of people who passed buckets of water to each other until they reached the fire, where the water was thrown onto the blaze. Obviously, this was not very effective, because there was usually too little water to stop the fire from spreading.

When fire engines, pulled by horses, were introduced in the late 18th century, the "bucket brigades" used to fill up their reservoirs, or stores, of water. This was dangerous. The pumps used were not very powerful, which meant bringing the engines too close to the fire, or at least as close as the terrified horses would allow. It was not until the 19th century that more powerful, steam-driven pumps and better water hoses began to be used.

WOMEN FIREFIGHTERS

Many women worked as firefighters in the "bucket brigades." One of them was an African-American slave named Molly Williams. In 1818, a fire broke out in New York during a blizzard, and Williams joined other firefighters to drag a fire engine through the deep snow to the site of the blaze.

At around the same time, Marina Betts, who was part French, part Indian, regularly took her place in "bucket brigade" lines, but her firefighting did not end there. There was always a big crowd watching fires, and Marina believed that "the menfolks should be working" to help put out the flames. So she used to ask men in the crowd to join in the firefighting and help fight the fire. However, if they refused to help, she threw a bucket of water over them!

DID YOU KNOW THAT...

• George Washington brought the first fire engine to America from England in 1765.

• Long before he became president, George Washington was a volunteer firefighter with the fire company in Alexandria, Virginia.

• Dalmatian dogs were used to guard engines and equipment when fire companies used to compete with each other to attend fires. This was because one way of getting the better of rivals was to steal or damage their equipment.

• The city of Znin in Poland, was either partly or completely destroyed by fire no less than six times—in 1447, 1494, 1688, 1692, 1700, and 1751.

THE GREAT CHICAGO FIRE OF 1871

Despite these advances, however, fire was a still a fearful destroyer. This was once again demonstrated in Chicago in October 1871, when a fierce blaze started in a barn owned by the O'Leary family in the northern part of the city. The fire quickly went out of control and spread throughout the city. The flames were soon swallowing up houses, buildings, and large mansions.

At this time, many homes were built of wood, and this fed the fire. The flames leapt across the Chicago River and, on the other side, set alight everything in its path. The inhabitants of Chicago fled, cramming the roads out of the city. Not all of them escaped unharmed: some 300 people were killed. Another 100,000, unfortunately, lost their homes.

George Washington, the first president of the United States, was very concerned about the danger of fire and was active in creating the first firefighting units in postcolonial America.

THE COW THAT STARTED A FIRE

It was said that a cow belonging to Mrs. O'Leary started the Great Chicago Fire of 1871, which destroyed the center of the city. A popular song was later written about it:

> Late one night, when we were all in bed,
> Mrs. O'Leary lit a lantern in the shed.
> Her cow kicked it over
> Then winked her eye and said:
> "There'll be a hot time in the old town tonight!"

FIREFIGHTING TODAY

Fortunately, firefighting methods are much more efficient today than they were in 1871. The use of high-tech equipment has greatly improved the firefighters' chances of controlling a blaze. Even so, the battle against fire continues, and there are more fire dangers than ever before. These can be caused by gas explosions in houses or faults in electrical equipment, such as television sets. Chemicals and other inflammable substances can leak from their containers and catch fire. In fact, you could say that firefighting is the longest war in history and that fire is one of the most difficult and dangerous enemies the world has ever faced.

These two German women are training to fight fires in the German city of Frankfurt during World War II. Heavy Allied bombing raids caused many fires during the later years of the war.

TRAINING TO BE A FIREFIGHTER

Firefighters must be well trained. The lives of people trapped in a fire depend on them. So do the lives of other members of their firefighting teams.

Everyone is afraid of fire—as they should be, considering the dangers. Firefighters, too, can be afraid, but they still have to do their job. They must do what most people would find terrifying: deliberately go near or into burning buildings and find their way past smoke and flames, collapsing ceilings, and unsafe floors to rescue **fire victims**. When the firefighters reach these victims, they must be calm and able to reassure them. They must stop victims from panicking so that they can lead them out of danger. Firefighters need great courage to do all this and they have to show that courage every time they attend a fire.

Even so, it is not enough for firefighters to be brave, healthy, and physically strong. They must also be properly trained, recognizing the dangers they face and knowing how their equipment works and how to use it. There is so much to learn, and firefighters will tell you this—that however long they have been in the fire service, they are always learning more.

Left: New York City firefighters carry a seriously injured person out of the rubble after the terrorist attack on the World Trade Center, September 11, 2001. More than 3,000 people died in the attacks.

New York City firefighters walk through the smoky remains searching for survivors. Thousands of lives were lost on September 11, 2001, when the World Trade Center's twin towers collapsed. A large number of those killed were firefighters and rescue workers.

WHAT FIREFIGHTERS HAVE TO KNOW

The first fact firefighters must learn is that saving lives is their most important task. At the scene of a blaze, firefighters will often use a telephone or radio to discusss the medical problems involved in saving someone's life. In fact, before you can even apply to be a firefighter, you must be able to show that you have studied emergency first aid, which means that you know how to stop bleeding, how to keep a fire victim's airway clear so that he or she can breathe, or how to move people with broken bones or spines so that they are not injured further.

This man survived a fire, but his home was destroyed. This is what his bedroom looked like afterward. More than 1.7 million fires are reported in the United States each year.

Firefighters have to be familiar with safety procedures, know how to put on protective clothing and take it off, and how to handle **breathing apparatus**. They must learn how to handle big, powerful hoses, learning how to control a hose when it is pumping water and keeping it directed into the fire. Because firefighters use special ropes and knots to pull victims safely out of burning buildings, they also need to know which knots to use and how to tie them.

Then there are the different kinds of fires they will fight: fires in automobiles, buses, and other vehicles; fires in wildlands, where the

A fire engine moves along a dusty road in California. In the background, the Manter Fire at the Sequoia National Forest can be seen continuing to burn. Luckily, the brewing storm clouds later provided enough rain to help firefighters contain the fire.

Two New York City firefighters wear breathing apparatus when tackling fires. This can often mean the difference between life and death among the noxious smoke and dust.

flames can spread rapidly, especially if the ground is dry and burns easily; fires in places where there are dangerous chemicals or other hazardous materials, which can explode if the flames reach them; and fires in high buildings, where firefighters have to use ladders and platforms to reach the victims.

Not all fires start by accident; sometimes, **arson** is involved. A fire started deliberately can easily burn out of control. At the end of 2001, bushfires destroyed large areas close to Sydney, Australia, even reaching the edges of the city itself. It was soon discovered that these fires were started by children and young people who had become

Firefighters battle a big fire in a warehouse in Worcester, Massachusetts. Six firemen died in this fire. It is estimated that in the United States, a person dies from a fire-related incident every 147 minutes.

bored during the school vacation. These irresponsible actions caused tremendous damage.

Arson, of course, is a crime, and arsonists have to be punished for it. So firefighters must always bear in mind that the fire they are fighting could have been deliberately started. Part of their training teaches them to watch out for signs of arson. In a building wrecked by fire, one of these signs might be an empty can of gas, particularly if it is found where a can of gas should not be. Another is the remains of matches or other means of lighting fires. While training,

Thanks to a fireman climbing high on his ladder, this elderly resident of a six-story building in Paris, France, was able to escape from danger and safely reach the ground.

firefighters learn how to recognize these signs and make sure that evidence of them is not disturbed: it could be important if the arsonist is caught and put on trial.

However, neither can you become a firefighter simply by studying at training courses or taking examinations. On-the-job training is important as well, so trainee firefighters go out with the fire engine teams to the scenes of fires and watch how they handle the emergency. By doing this, trainees can see what the scene of a real fire is like and experience firefighting for themselves.

Tired, grim-faced firefighters take a well-earned rest from fighting the fires in New York City. The New York City Fire Department responds to more than 60,000 structural fires each year.

THE FIRE POLICE

Some firefighters are police officers as well, so they have to train and study twice as hard to do their job. The scene of a fire is always dangerous, but the firefighters and their engines and equipment can face extra problems.

Relatives of fire victims can become terrified when they see what is happening to their loved ones, so the **fire police** have to be there to control them and make sure they do not make the emergency worse.

Quite often, too, large crowds of spectators gather when a fire breaks out, either to share the excitement of watching the blaze or for some other, less innocent, reason. This is where the fire police come in. They are there to stop people from damaging fire engines or stealing things from them. The crowd may also create difficulties by getting too near to the fire or blocking the road that leads to the scene, which means the fire engines and firefighters cannot get through to the fire. It is the job of the fire police to keep the crowd at a safe distance from a fire. This is often for the spectators' own safety, too, because anything can happen at a fire scene— explosions, debris falling from the burning building, or poisonous fumes or dangerous chemicals escaping from their containers.

REACTIONS

Some would-be firefighters have romantic ideas about the job. To them, it is exciting and they see themselves as great heroes, valiantly battling the flames and admired by all for doing so. Firefighters are certainly heroes, but their job is not the least bit romantic. Fires are horrifying, and destruction by fire is a fearful sight, for both victims and firefighters. People who cannot face up to these realities are not suited to be firefighters, and this is what some trainees discover when they attend a real fire.

THE SIZE UP

Another important lesson for trainee firefighters to learn is what the fire services call the "size up." **Sizing up** is understanding what must

be done at the scene of a fire, and every fire is different. For instance, how does the location of a fire affect the way it must be fought? A blaze that starts in open country, with plenty of space around it and probably no other buildings that might also catch fire, is completely different from a fire in a city street, where the buildings are close together.

What is the time of day or night when the fire station receives news of the alarm? If it is a daytime fire, there will be a lot of traffic in the surrounding streets, together with parked automobiles and a large number of people. Obviously, this creates problems. On the other hand, daytime also brings an advantage. Many people are likely to see the fire and raise the alarm, so the fire service can respond quickly. In contrast, if the fire happens at

Three firefighters in Los Angeles are called to an emergency. In the United States, there is a fire-related injury every 24 minutes.

FIREFIGHTERS AND THEIR FAMILIES

Firefighters know that they may be killed or injured when they are fighting fires. So when anyone volunteers to become a firefighter, their families become closely involved.

Volunteer Firefighter's Poem

We are volunteers, we don't get paid for what we do

But our hope and prayers are to always see you through

We can be eating or awakened in the middle of the night

With a blast of our pagers saying, "There is a fire we need to fight!"

We are up and dressed and out the door

We meet sirens blaring and trucks that roar

The adrenaline pumping, we're ready to go

Will we make it home? We never know.

Our jobs are to fight fires and to also save a life

Our goal is to make it home to our children and our wife

We do the unexpected. We tread where people fear.

night, the streets will be less busy. This helps, in a way, because there are fewer people in danger and the road to the fire scene is clearer. Yet there is an added problem with a nighttime fire. With fewer people to see it, a night fire in an empty building (for example, a closed department store) might be burning for quite a while before anyone notices it. As a result, the fire is likely to have done a lot of damage before the firefighters reach it.

What is the weather like? What is the state of the water supply for

Another poem is entitled, *I Am a Fireman's Wife*

The table's set, the meal's prepared,

Our guest will soon arrive.

My husband once more disappears,

with the hope of keeping a child alive.

While waiting at home alone, our plans have gone awry.

My first response is to sit right down and cry.

But soon again I realize the importance of my life

When I agreed to take on the duties of being a Fireman's Wife.

While there may be drawbacks, I'll take them in my stride.

Knowing "My Daddy saved a life,"

our children can say with pride.

The gusting winds and raging flames may be his final fate.

But with God's help, I can remain my fireman's faithful mate.

(Anonymous)

fighting the fire? How tall is the burning building and on which floor did the fire start? How far has it spread? Is it safe to use fire-axes to break down doors or walls, or has the fire so weakened these structures that there could be a dangerous collapse?

These are just some of the many questions firefighters must ask themselves when sizing up. Once finished, they must be confident they know what to do. They cannot afford to think twice or make a mistake; someone might die if they do.

FIRES IN THE CITY

Today, millions of people live in cities, and that means hundreds of thousands of houses, apartment buildings, offices, schools, theaters, hospitals, hotels, department stores, and streets crowded with automobiles and buses. Fighting fires in cities presents a unique set of problems.

The first problem is getting fire engines to the scene of the fire as quickly as they can. This is why the engines sound loud alarms as they race through the streets and are allowed to drive through red traffic lights, while all other traffic has to stop. Engines do not have time to wait for the green light.

GETTING TO A FIRE

Getting to a fire can mean driving several engines through the city streets. Two engines and one escape ladder may be all that is needed for a blaze in a single house, but larger buildings may require up to four engines and two ladders, or even more.

Fortunately, firefighters are good at finding their way around their own cities. They know where to find short-

Left: "Ground Zero" was the name given to the World Trade Center after it collapsed in September 2001. The shock of the devastation can be seen in the faces of these New York City firefighters.

cuts through the back streets and how the streets join up with each other. They also know where to find the **fire hydrants**. The hydrant—a word that comes from the ancient Greek "hudor," meaning water—is a water pipe linked to a city's main water supply. Hydrants have nozzles to which firefighters can attach their hoses.

In the best scenario, firefighters can get hold of the plans, or already know the layout, of the building that is on fire. However, this is not always possible, especially in poorer city districts. Even so, firefighters are familiar with the way fires behave and know in advance what they are likely to find when they reach the scene. Fire spreads upward, so a blaze on one floor of an apartment will soon spread to the apartment directly above it. Stairways are ready-made spaces for fire to climb up the inside of a building, so leaving the building that way is often impossible. Fire ladders placed against the outside walls must be used to enable the inhabitants to escape.

In addition, buildings are all-too-frequently constructed in ways that make it easy for fire to spread. For instance, the kitchen and bathroom are two rooms where there is a special danger of fire. In a big apartment building, these are often built one on top of the other. As a result, there are pipes that run up a building from the first floor to the top floor and, like stairways, these can help a fire reach upward through the building in a short time.

Left: Some buildings close to the World Trade Center were badly affected by the collapse of the twin towers. Here, firefighters combat smoldering remains that are still burning by using an aerial ladder to reach the uppermost part of the wreckage.

MULTIPLE DWELLINGS AND PRIVATE DWELLINGS

At the scene of a fire, a firefighter's first thought must be: how many people are in danger? In cities, this usually means quite a large number. Buildings in which many people live are not necessarily skyscrapers; they are normally **multiple dwellings** no more than three or four stories high, housing three or more families. Firefighters have to assume that not everyone in the building will know it is on fire. So the first thing they do is search the floor where the fire has broken out and the floors above it. That way, they have a better chance of finding and rescuing the inhabitants, even if they have to wake them up in bed, get them out of the bathroom, or tell them to leave the building even though they are in the middle of eating a meal.

WAYS TO FIGHT THE FIRE

Ways to fight a fire can vary, depending on the equipment that is closest at hand. Suppose a television set, stove, or piece of furniture has burst into flames. People are advised to buy one or more **fire extinguishers** and place them in a prominent position in their rooms, so that they can grab them and use them as soon as a fire starts—but not everyone takes this advice. Even if there is a fire extinguisher in the building, it may be too far away. By the time someone retrieves it, the whole room, or the entire apartment or floor, could be on fire. The officer in charge of the firefighting team may not be able to stop this from happening; but what he can do is order that a hose, which is much larger and more powerful than the average extinguisher, be brought up with all possible speed.

Most of the homes in which fires occur are not multiple dwellings. Fire is more likely to break out in **private dwellings**, where only one or two families live. They usually start on the first floor or in the basement, because this is where the equipment that causes most fires is likely to be found—stoves for cooking meals, the electricity supply, or the water heater. Another cause of fire is cigarettes. Many people smoke in their living rooms and bedrooms, and all it takes to start a fire is for a smoker to fall asleep and let a lighted cigarette drop on the carpet, furniture, or bedclothes.

Italian firefighters deal with a blaze on a street in the city of Milan. A gas explosion caused this fire and destruction. Fire departments throughout the world regularly carry out inspections of buildings and appliances to ensure that they are safe and not a fire hazard.

HOUSE FIRES

In Britain, in 2002, it was reckoned that 80 out of every 100 fires were caused by lighted cigarette ends. At first, the danger of fire might not seem too serious. For several minutes, the cigarette end smolders, burning slowly and giving off smoke, but as yet, no flames. But almost everything in a room is inflammable, that is, capable of catching fire, and the flames soon follow. Suddenly, the fire explodes into a big blaze and spreads rapidly. The use of plastics in some furniture, like mattresses, means that fire will produce choking, poisonous clouds of smoke. It is the smoke that kills, and that is why getting victims out of a room on fire is of first importance for firefighters.

To help the victims escape to safety, the firefighters must make sure that the water supply is flowing properly to let them fight the

House fires cause terrible damage. This one occurred in Montana, where the house next door caught fire, too. A lot of people had their property destroyed that day.

In a fire this high up in a building, it is a long way down to the ground. Only the firemen's skill and equipment can enable fire victims to escape unharmed.

fire. After that, they place a hose in position to protect the bedroom doors, because the bedroom is where most people trapped by fire are found.

VENT, ENTER, SEARCH

Finally, the firefighters perform what is called the **VES** routine. VES stands for "vent, enter, search." To vent a room, the windows are broken so that heat and smoke can escape. All shades, venetian blinds, and drapes, which could keep heat and smoke from getting out, are pulled away, and a ladder is placed at the side of the window to let the people inside climb down to safety.

"Enter" and "Search" mean going into the rooms and searching

WITNESS TO A CITY FIRE

Around midnight on December 6, 1997, Jill Druse, daughter of a firefighter and wife of a newspaper reporter, went with her husband to the scene of a serious fire in Niles, Michigan. Even before they arrived, the fire had spread throughout the building, and the firefighters were in a great deal of danger. Jill watched them and later wrote of how much she admired them.

"I stood there and thought how selfless these men and women must be to risk their own lives in order to save someone else's [property]. I watched the men inside the building fight the smoke in order to dowse the fire. I also [realized] how much respect I have for all those men and women who strap on an air pack and go into a smoke-filled building never knowing if they will ever come out."

INSIDE A BURNING BUILDING

In his book, *Report from Engine Company 82,* Dennis Smith, a New York City firefighter in the South Bronx district, described how he fought a fire inside a burning building.

The fire was blazing away in three rooms at the end of the hall, and the smoke was so thick that Smith and another firefighter had to lie flat on the floor in order to find enough air to breathe. They managed to break down the door leading to one of the rooms and then directed their water hose inside to extinguish the flames. There was a loud sound of fire crackling, and as the water jet dislodged some plaster from the ceiling, pieces of it fell to the floor, hissing and steaming.

The fire, started deliberately by three young arsonists, was eventually put out, but two people died and another was badly injured. This was more than a fire: it was double homicide.

them for any people who might be trapped inside. Sometimes, fire victims may be affected by the smoke and fumes, in which case, the firefighters will adminsiter first aid. Once the VES routine is completed, the firefighters can concentrate on putting out the fire and making the building safe.

You can see from all this that there is much more to fighting fires than simply pouring on large amounts of water. Firefighters must first save lives. A fire may be put out, but firefighters have failed in their duty if afterward, among the ashes, they find the bodies of victims they should have saved.

Suspended high up in the air from a crane fitted to a fire engine, these firemen face tremendous danger as they fight a huge fire. You cannot afford to be afraid of heights in this job.

CITY FIRES AROUND THE WORLD

Each year, more fires break out in private dwellings than in big buildings. In 2000, private dwellings accounted for 72 percent of the total 380,000 home fires that firefighters had to tackle in the United States. At least 3,420 people were killed and another 16,475 were injured. Between 1994 and 1998, most people killed in fires died between 10:00 P.M. and 6:00 A.M., even though only one-quarter of all home fires happened between those hours. December, January, and February were the worst months for fires because it was then, during the winter, that the heating was on in homes while people were asleep in bed.

The first sign of a fire is often the smoke it creates. However, despite a lot of advertising and advice from fire prevention authorities, four-fifths of all home fire deaths between 1989 and 1998 occurred in homes where smoke alarms had not been installed. And where there is smoke, you will usually find a fire.

Buenos Aires, the capital of Argentina, is one of the most crowded cities on earth—13,775,993 inhabitants in 2001. The population of Mexico City, capital of Mexico, is almost as great—13,096,686 inhabitants in 2000. Other big cities have smaller populations, but this still means a large number of people; for example, in 2000, there were 3,694,820 living in Los Angeles and 2,643,581 in Rome, Italy. Three of these cities (Mexico City, Tokyo, and Los Angeles) lie in earthquake zones. Serious earthquakes—measuring 6 or more on the Richter earthquake scale—not only wreck large areas of a city and kill people, but can also start fires.

This fire completely wrecked the beautiful Fenice opera house in Venice, Italy, in 1996. However, the building had already been rebuilt once, having burned to the ground in 1836.

WILDLAND FIRES

Nature can be very cruel. In the beautiful scenery of the wildlands, there lurk many possible dangers. Wildfires are just one, and they can inflict dreadful damage. For the reason that the wildlands are wild and unpopulated, there may be no one to notice a wildfire until it has taken hold over a large area.

The heat of summer can dry out the trees, leaves, and twigs, making it easier for a fire to break out. Careless visitors to the **wildlands** may easily start a fire, either by throwing a still-burning cigarette end away on dry brushwood, or by failing to put out a campfire properly. Even a small piece of glass is dangerous. When the sun's rays shine on it, the glass concentrates the heat, and this can be enough to set alight brushwood, sticks, or vegetation.

DANGEROUS THUNDERSTORMS

Thunderstorms over the wildlands are particularly dangerous. A powerful bolt of lightning, with a temperature as high as 60,000°F (33,316°C), may strike just a single tree, bringing it crashing to the ground. As it falls, however, tiny flames may be burning inside it.

Left: "Thank You Firefighters" says this notice put up at the scene of a wildland fire. These fires are probably the most difficult to deal with, because they burn over such a wide area.

Smoke towers over a burning mountainside in the Cleveland Forest, near Temecula, California, in August 2000. The fire consumed more than 11,000 acres (4,450 hectares) of woodland.

SPOTTING FIRES FROM FAR AWAY

Weather conditions have an important effect on the chances of fire breaking out, especially in the wildlands. Watching the weather is the work of the 1,500 Remote Automated Weather Stations (**RAWS**) found all over the United States. Most of these stations are in the western states, where the chance of wildfires is greatest. In the East Bay Hills area of California, for instance, wildfires broke out 15 times between 1923 and 1991—and 1991 saw two separate fires that threatened both the wildlands and the towns of the region.

The RAWS weather reports are delivered to National Interagency Fire Center (NIFC) computers by way of the Geostationary Operational Environmental Satellite (GOES). Firefighters use this information to make their own forecasts of what the wildfires may do. They can then make sure they have the necessary resources to fight them.

These can transfer themselves to dry vegetation. Before long, from this small beginning, an entire forest is ablaze.

Fortunately, weather forecasters can predict the arrival of thunderstorms over the wildlands. They can also identify those that have the greatest chance of starting a fire. In addition, the progress of lightning strikes can be tracked by computer; aircraft then fly over the area to check for smoke or flames.

Low- as well as high-tech methods can be used in detecting **wildfires**. In remote forests, tall fire towers have been built with

The U.S. Search and Rescue Task Force (SARTF) deals with fires, rescue, and emergencies in all the wildland areas of the United States.

observation platforms at the top. From these platforms, observers can see for miles around as they watch for signs of wildfire.

Sometimes, a fire can be left to burn itself out, but others are far too dangerous for that. Detecting big wildfires early is important, as is assessing the size of the blaze. Often, a serious wildfire is far too huge for local firefighting teams to handle, and others have to be called in from surrounding areas, sometimes from all over the country. Teams fighting wildfires can become utterly exhausted from the effort, not least because the fires so often seem to be one jump ahead of them. Fire can leap across roads and swamps and, if large enough, across lakes as well.

Wildfires also have an ally—the wind, which can direct the flames to fresh places, and so firefighters are faced with yet another

Right: This helicopter released a 500-gallon (2,273-liter) bucket of water on a wildfire at the High Meadow near Pine in Colorado on June 16, 2000. Fighting fires from the air is often the most effective way of containing wildland fires without putting lives at risk.

blaze to handle. In addition, there is no supply of piped water in the wildlands, so water must be carried to the scene of the fire. Aircraft were first used in firefighting in California in 1919. If there is a lake near the fire scene, aircraft will scoop up water and transport it to the firefighters. Helicopters can hover over a lake while a hose is dropped into the water; this is a suction hose that sucks the water

Firefighters come from all over the U.S. to fight fires in other states. In August 2000, these firemen were brought in from the National Guard at Fort Hood, Texas, to fight a fire in the barren hillside in the Payette National Forest near Bergdorf Junction, Idaho.

WILDFIRE DAMAGE

The months of May and June 1998 were unusually hot and dry in Florida. As a result, wildland fires broke out over many parts of the state. The situation was so serious that every one of the state's counties was declared a disaster area.

The damage was enormous. Around 26,000 acres (10,530 hectares) of farmland were burned. Farmers in northern Florida lost $80,000 worth of crops—corn, peanuts, cotton, watermelons, and soybeans. The heat of the fires ruined more crops, worth another $100 million. At least one person died and some 30 people were injured, most of them from smoke inhalation or from burns.

Every day, around 80 new fires broke out, most of them caused by lightning. Some 500,000 acres (202,500 hectares) of forest were destroyed, and the smoke from the wildfire blotted out the sun as far away as Miami, 250 miles (402 km) distant. Fires reached towns and burned some 100 homes. Huge **palls** of smoke hung over Jacksonville, Daytona Beach, Tallahassee, and Orlando. In Jacksonville, 600 inhabitants were ordered to leave their homes, and another 150 in the town of Hampton were forced to do the same. Near the town of Waldo, the blaze stretched over a distance of seven miles (11 km); fortunately, before it reached the town, the wind shifted and kept the flames away.

Although firefighters rushed to Florida from all over the United States, they were not able to put out the fires. All they could do was to contain them; that is, make sure they spread no further before, eventually, they burned themselves out.

into a tank built into the underside of the helicopters. Helicopters also have their own water tanks or use big scoops, known as buckets, which can hold up to 400 gallons (1,820 liters) of water.

Helicopters and aircraft can also bring pumps or hoses and other equipment directly to the firefighters on the ground. In other aircraft, pilots fly over the area of wildland on fire and keep the ground crews informed about how quickly it is spreading and in

Two firefighters from the Forestry Service of Sequoia National Forest in California stand in front of a mass of burning trees in 1999. Some fires are too big to put out. Sometimes, all the firefighters can do is contain the fire and wait for it to burn itself out.

When wood burns, it burns fiercely, and wildland fires can easily leap from one tree to the next until the whole forest is on fire. Alaska suffered unusually severe fires in 2000, with more than a million acres (404,600 hectares) being affected.

what direction. In addition, the helicopters and aircraft can fight the fire themselves by dropping their cargo of water directly onto the flames. They may also drop "slurry," a fire retardant that slows the progress of a fire by reducing the supply of oxygen that lets the flame burn. Aircraft will often spray it all over a forest.

THE HOTSHOTS

The people who fight wildland fires are often known as **hotshots**, and there may be hundreds of them tackling the blaze from the

National Guard firefighters douse flames near a residential district of Los Alamos, New Mexico, in 2000.

ground. They construct "fire lines" by taking away leaves or branches lying at the edge of the fire, then beating out the flames and spraying water on them: this helps keep the fire on the other side of the "line." The hotshots use radios to report the progress of the fire, and aircraft follow its path, sometimes using thermal imaging cameras, which record the intensity of the heat in a variety of colors.

The temperatures the cameras record can be phenomenally high—as much as 2,000°F (1,093°C), and the hotshots have to be alert to many other dangers in a fire area. In hilly country, boulders can become dislodged and come tumbling down the hillsides toward them. Flaming branches, known as "snags," may topple down from burning trees. If the smoke from the fire is extremely thick, the firefighters will have to crawl on their knees or lie flat on the ground, where there is some breathable air to be found.

TRAPPED BY FIRE

Sometimes, the firefighters themselves become trapped by a wildland fire. The blaze is all around them, the smoke chokes them, they feel they cannot breathe—but there is no obvious way out. Their

These firefighters are carrying their own water, contained in the canisters on their backs. In the year 2000, there were 79,000 separate wildland fires across the United States.

only chance is to protect themselves from the flames or be consumed and die. In case this happens, firefighters attending wildland fires carry a fire shelter—a small tent made of aluminum foil and fiberglass specially made to keep away the flames, heat, and smoke. Once inside this tent, firefighters are able to survive, even when surrounded by the fire, and can wait until the blaze passes by. Then, they can safely emerge.

SMOKEJUMPERS AND RAPPELERS

When fires break out deep inside a forest, and as long as they are still relatively small, some firefighters, known as **smokejumpers**, parachute down into the area of the blaze. This is truly daredevil firefighting and it has to be done skillfully, or smokejumpers can be badly injured.

First of all, the aircraft pilot has to choose the area into which the smokejumpers are going to parachute. Then, streamers are dropped so that the pilot can observe which way the winds are blowing. If they are blowing the fire toward the chosen target area, the smokejumpers cannot use it.

If the winds are favorable, the smokejumpers' heavy equipment is parachuted down, and the smokejumpers follow. Sometimes, they have to "thread the needle," which means going in to land among the trees. This is why smokejumpers wear special protective helmets with masks attached: they can be injured while coming down through the branches.

If the smokejumpers are falling too fast and need to slow down,

Fighting a wildland fire is a long and exhausting business. Hotshots may have to work for up to 40 hours at a stretch. Even after a fire seems to be out, there is always the chance that a few tiny flames are still burning, ready to start yet another blaze. So the firefighters have to search around, sniffing the air for the smell of smoke and digging up small fires still burning underground and putting them out with water.

they may have to do something really tricky—a "tree jump." The tree jump means coming down among the treetops so that the parachute gets caught in the branches. This, of course, stops the smokejumpers from crashing to the ground, but leaves them hanging high above it. They then use a rope to lower themselves down to the ground.

Rappelers—the firefighters who carry out "rap attacks"—do not use parachutes. Instead, they use ropes suspended from a helicopter hovering up to 300 feet (90 m) from the ground. The special body harness they wear enables them to slide down the rope at a comfortable speed and, like the smokejumpers, they also wear protective helmets.

As they come in to land by rope, rappelers can seem a strange sight. They need hard hats to tackle fires, so they strap them to their legs and also carry bags containing equipment tied to their harnesses. Heavier equipment, like saws or pumps, can also be lowered down to the ground by a rope.

AIRCRAFT ON FIRE

Flying is often cited as the safest way to travel. One reason for this is that aircraft designers and manufacturers, as well as the airlines that carry millions of people around the world, have always been careful about safety. On board an aircraft, the passengers' seats are made of fireproof fabric, which burns less easily in a fire, or not at all. There are also smoke detectors, heat sensors, water sprinklers, and fire extinguishers for the crew to use.

If fire breaks out in places that cannot be reached—like the cargo hold or the fuel tanks, which are carried inside the wings—aircraft carry a supply of foam that can be used to flood these areas and put out the fire.

Before a flight takes off from an airport, passengers are shown how to put on life jackets in case the plane crashes into the sea. They also learn about using the oxygen masks the plane carries so that they will be able to breathe if the plane's outside "skin" is punctured, causing the pressure inside to drop.

When it comes to precautions against fire and other emergencies, the airlines try to anticipate what can go wrong and take steps in advance to prevent it. Unfortunately, accidents do happen, no

Left: New York City firefighters search the rubble of the twin towers, September 2001. The wreckage of the two aircraft that crashed into the World Trade Center is buried somewhere here among the rubble and carnage.

Firefighters work to put out a fire after a Cuban airliner crashed in Quito, Ecuador, in August 1998.

matter how many precautions are taken. The fact that flying is considered the safest form of travel certainly means that the risk of fire or other accident has been reduced, but not that it has been completely eliminated.

ACCIDENTS WILL HAPPEN

Tragically, air crashes can cause multiple victims, but such a disaster is by no means inevitable. If an aircraft crashes at or near an airport, rescue and firefighting teams are already there to deal with it.

The teams at airports are usually small. This is not just because it

The World Trade Center towers stood for just an hour after the two aircraft were crashed into them. The fires started by the aviation fuel on board the aircraft soon ate into the buildings and caused them to collapse.

DID YOU KNOW THAT ...

When ships in harbor catch fire, fireboats are used to suck up water and throw it at the flames?

Members of the crew on board ships are specially trained to deal with fires and hold regular fire drills?

Railroad trains have special detectors fitted underneath the cars to look for signs of overheating that can start a fire?

Along a railroad track, there are hotbox detectors that check all the cars passing along the rails for signs of overheating?

When fire breaks out in an underground train, pipes called "dry drops" reach up to water hydrants in the street above?

is rare for aircraft to crash or make crash-landings on runways. Often, the traffic controllers at an airport know that an aircraft is in trouble because they are in contact with the pilot; so other teams can be alerted before the airplane tries to land.

Once alerted, the teams do not wait for the crash to occur. As

Right: Firefighters pour foam over an aircraft that crashed at Sarajevo Airport in Bosnia, on October 8, 1999. All major international airports are equipped with firefighting units to deal with the potential of fires onboard aircraft.

soon as they learn of the emergency, they race across to the runway, monitoring the airplane's progress by radio. The teams use special vehicles to take them quickly to where the crash may take place. The most important are the foam pumpers, which carry pumps that can fight an aircraft fire using special foam. Foam is used because the aviation fuel used by aircraft causes hydrocarbon fires, which burn much more fiercely than the ordinary fuel in automobiles. Water alone cannot usually handle an aviation fuel fire.

THE FOAM PUMPERS

There are several of these foam-pumping vehicles. One is the rapid-intervention vehicle, which is quite fast and normally reaches the

This Thai Airways Boeing 737 was consumed by fire and burned out while standing on the tarmac at Bangkok airport. The aircraft burst into flames only minutes before passengers were due to go aboard.

CONCORDE CRASHES NEAR PARIS

Air accidents can be caused by events no one can forecast. Such was the case when an Air France Concorde airliner crashed near Paris, France, after taking off for New York on July 25, 2000. All 109 passengers and crew and four people on the ground were killed.

Afterward, investigators discovered that a small piece of metal had fallen onto the runway from a Continental Airlines DC-10 "jumbo" jet that had taken off a few minutes previously. The metal ripped through one of the Concorde's tires, and debris from the tire hit one of the supersonic airliner's fuel tanks. The tank ruptured and the fuel ignited, setting the aircraft on fire.

Air France and British Airways, who also use Concorde, grounded their entire fleet. Before they were allowed to fly again, the Concordes were fitted with new extra-strength tires and the insides of their fuel tanks were strengthened with a material called Kevlar; Kevlar is also used to make bulletproof vests.

After these improvements were made, the first Concorde to fly again took off from Paris for New York on November 8, 2001. The flight was successful and experienced no incidents.

scene of the aircraft fire before the others. Larger foam pumpers can spray foam higher and further—over a distance of about 75 yards (82 m)—using their tall turrets. There are also ground-sweep nozzles that spray foam all over the runway around the crashed airplane. This, as well as the foam and water that is sprayed over the **fuselage** to cool the aircraft down, makes it safer for passengers to escape through a special corridor that stretches down to the ground from the airplane's exit doors.

Some foam pumpers are so powerful that they can punch a hole in the aircraft's fuselage and pour their foam through it to put out any flames that are burning inside. If an aircraft has crashed at night, or if there is a lot smoke swirling around, foam pumpers may also carry infrared cameras. This camera enables the rescuers and firefighters to "see" through the dark and smoke.

Aircraft are often constructed from lightweight metals, such as

New York City firefighters battle the flames. In New York City, there are more than 11,000 uniformed firefighters and fire officers, along with 2,500 paramedics and 200 fire marshals. They respond to more than 60,000 fires each year.

Firefighters search the wreckage of the World Trade Center after the terrorist attack. Work clearing the wreckage at Ground Zero continued for many months after the terrible terrorist attack of September 11, 2001.

titanium, which is, unfortunately, highly flammable. To combat this, the teams carry extinguishers specially made for extinguishing titanium fires. They may also pump dry chemicals over the aircraft to help put out the flames.

Fires in a crashed aircraft are not the only blazes firefighters have to worry about. The crash may have caused fuel to leak out onto the ground, where it starts its own fire; foam and water have to be used to extinguish this fire before it can spread. Foam is particularly effective because it starves the fire of oxygen.

Putting out a fire on board a ship loaded with dangerous nitric acid on the Rhine River near Düsseldorf, Germany on November 21, 2001. Firemen feared the ship would sink and pollute the river.

SAVING LIVES

As with all firefighting, the first thing to do is save lives—in this case, the lives of the passengers and crew. If the rescue teams have to enter the aircraft, they wait until the people stop coming out down the escape corridors. Of course, there may be injured passengers still inside the plane, but the teams have to be careful before going inside to search. If, for example, the aircraft's doors will not open, the teams may have to cut holes in the fuselage, and this will let air into the aircraft, which may cause fresh fires to start inside.

**Firemen of the New York Fire Department at the scene of a fire.
Each year in New York City, there are more than 900,000 fire
apparatus responses to fires, medical calls, and other emergencies.**

The inside of a crashed aircraft is a terrible mess, scattered with debris, luggage, and food carts. The rescuers and firefighters have to work their way through it all to make sure no one remains who is injured or who has been left behind. Even after the fires are out and the passengers and crew have gone, a crashed aircraft remains a danger. It may be soaked in aviation fuel, which can easily burst

DISASTER IN NEW YORK CITY: WHY DID THE TWIN TOWERS COLLAPSE?

You only have to say the date—September 11, 2001—and everybody knows what you are talking about: the terrorist attacks on New York City and Washington, D.C.

In New York City, the targets of the Al Quaeda terrorists and their leader, Osama bin Laden, were the soaring twin towers of the World Trade Center. Both towers eventually collapsed. The south tower went first, 45 minutes after the attack, and the north tower fell after 105 minutes. Within a matter of moments, more than 3,000 people are thought to have died. Only five people were found alive in the wreckage.

Why did the towers collapse? There are two main reasons. The first is that the tanks on board the aircraft were carrying a huge amount of aviation fuel—around 2,400 gallons (8,800 ls) each—for long flights across the United States. This fuel ignited on impact with the towers, causing an enormous fire that reached temperatures of more than 2,700°F (1,482°C).

The second reason is the way in which the World Trade Center

into flames while the wreckage is being removed for examination.

For this reason, the firefighters have to remain on standby for as long as investigators are at the scene. It is important for investigators to have a thorough look at the wreckage, because it provides clues about the cause of the crash. And these clues can help make sure that other aircraft do not suffer the same fate in the future.

was built. Prior to 1966, which is when construction on the World Trade Center began, most skyscrapers, in New York and elsewhere in the world, had been built around a frame and were constructed of masonry, or stonework. The twin towers had no masonry and no frame. Instead, they had a tube structure, which meant that they were made of hollow steel columns: floor trusses, or struts, about 1.5 inches (4 cm) thick, extended from the outside of the towers to their center. This gave them much more floor space for offices than the masonry-built skyscrapers—as much as 40,000 square feet (4,860 sq m) extra per floor.

Tragically, however, this extra space helped the fire to spread rapidly and also incinerated people inside until there was nothing left of them. Once the floors and the struts beneath them melted in the intense heat, the tubular columns began to give way. Soon after, the floors collapsed, one on top of the other, until the whole building had crashed to the ground in a mess of rubble and debris.

The magnificent twin towers, the pride of the New York City skyline, had become the wasteland known as **Ground Zero**.

FIREFIGHTING IN THE FUTURE

Today, technology progresses so fast that it often seems the future has already arrived. Modern firefighters now make use of an array of sophisticated equipment, and even the methods of firefighting are changing.

Firefighters wear new helmets made of light materials. They use cell phones, computers, satellites, and thermal imaging. Fire pumps now have gauges that do their own calculations to tell firefighters how fast they must pump water to put out the fire. A substance called Class A Foam is mixed with the water to extinguish fires faster than water alone and to keep the fire scene cooler for longer. The emergency medical services use the "doc in a box," a camera that can be plugged in inside a building where there is a fire victim. A doctor then looks at the picture on a TV screen and can recommend the appropriate treatment.

New firefighting methods are also being developed. For instance, instead of chopping a hole in a wall or door with a hatchet to see what is happening inside, firefighters will use instruments that can detect heat in a building. Sometimes, heat comes from people or animals; sometimes from a fire. The instruments will let the

Left: Wildland fires are a problem in many parts of the world, and countries such as the United States, Canada, and Australia have developed technology and systems to deal with this ever-present threat.

Aircraft specially equipped to spray vast amounts of water over wildlands on fire will be used extensively in the future.

SHAPE-SHIFTING ICE ROBOTS

In the future, shape-shifting robots made of ice or of plates bolted to a frame will be used to fight fires. Firefighters will send the ice robots into a fire to melt over the blaze and reduce it or put it out.

Other robots are made from several interconnected cubes, which lets them change their shape. These robots are enormously strong. If a ceiling in a burning building looks like it will collapse, they can be sent in to hold it up.

firefighters identify the heat source without having to make holes in walls, which may damage the building or put themselves or others at extra risk.

WEARING SENSORS

Knowing how fast a fire is spreading is an important part of the firefighter's job. Up to now, they have mostly used their own experience to judge the rate of progress. This, no matter how experienced they are, can only be a matter of guesswork—but not any more. Before long, firefighters will carry sensors on their visors or their clothing to tell them about heat and smoke levels, the direction of the wind, or the amount of poisonous fumes or harmful radiation produced by the fire. They may also carry small computers that will help them monitor the progress of a fire.

Advanced technology and new ways to use it will also be able to improve detection of those most-extensive and difficult-to-handle fires—the wildfires that can spread so rapidly through forests and woods. Wildland fires are often considered to be the firefighter's greatest and most dangerous challenge. They flare up quietly, usually out of sight; start new fires even while the existing ones are being fought; create enormous damage; and in some cases, threaten cities and towns, their homes, and inhabitants.

Sometimes, nature will come to the rescue and put out the flames with rain. This happened in 2001 when over 400 forest fires in northern Alberta, Canada, were under control, but not yet extinguished. The rain helped to put them out, but not before nearly 600 square miles (1,554 sq km) of land had been destroyed and hundreds of people had been forced to leave their homes.

THE AERIAL MOBILE MAPPING SYSTEM

Waiting for rain is not a satisfactory solution for firefighters, especially since it is often the absence of rainfall that helps wildland fires start in the first place. Far better to use technology, which, unlike rainfall, can be controlled and directed at the fire. This is what Dr. Naser El-Sheimy of the University of Calgary, in Alberta, Canada, thought when he devised his Aerial Mobile Mapping System (**AMMS**). AMMS is not, in itself, new technology; what it does is use existing ways of firefighting and modern equipment and combines them with high-tech modern communications. Between them, these can detect remote, hidden "hotspots" in forests, which, if unnoticed and unattended, soon grow into big, serious fires.

AMMS works like this. The pilots of aircraft are provided with thermal (heat-seeking) cameras able to detect infrared radiation from a hotspot. As the aircraft flies over a forest, these cameras can pick up heat patterns, making it possible to find out exactly where the hotspots are. AMMS does need to be developed further. For instance, in June 2001, the system was still investigating how hotspots become big fires and how long it takes them to do so. In time, it is hoped, AMMS will be able to perform the most vital task in wildfire fighting: stopping forest fires before they have a chance to get going in earnest.

City fires, of course, present an opposite problem from fires in the wildlands, where fire can work away unseen, destroying large

This is what some of the western U.S. states look like on the Aerial Mobile Mapping System. As the picture shows, a heavy fire rages in a wildland area of New Mexico.

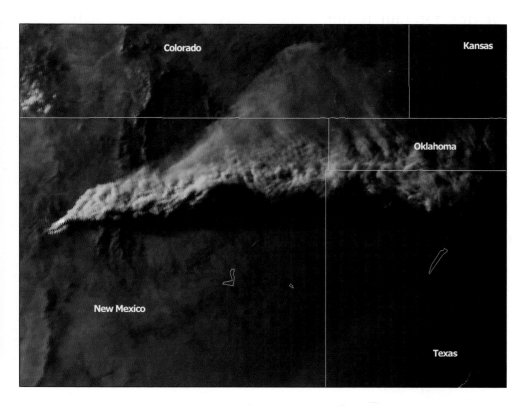

AUSTRALIA: FIREFIGHTING BY COMPUTER

In Australia, the New South Wales Fire Brigades (NSWFB) and the Science and Technology Laboratory of the Commonwealth Scientific and Industrial Research Organization (CSIRO) have undertaken a lot of computerized research. They have built up a big database, known as AIRS—the Australian Incident Reporting System—using information from a million or more fires that have occurred since 1990. This provides a wide-ranging picture of how fires spread, how hazardous materials behave in fire situations, how to rescue fire victims, and every other detail involved in fire emergencies. All this information can be accessed as a guide to fighting future fires.

The database also provides the chance for further research. For instance, firefighters may report on the thickness or the height of walls or the strength of a fire door in a house. This information can then be used to examine the structure of buildings, which may lead to new designs that provide better protection.

Computers and other high-tech equipment may make organizing firefighting more efficient, but the flames will still have to be fought by firefighters confronting the blaze with their hoses. This Australian firefighter is battling a wildland blaze in New South Wales.

uninhabited stretches of territory. The problem with city fires, as mentioned, is that there can be too many people around, thus increasing the danger of death or injury. In a shopping mall, for example, where a lot of people may be trapped inside, it can be difficult for firefighters to know what is going on. In the future, they will be able to use an infrared-color zoom lens fixed to a ladder to show them the scene.

Even fire training will benefit from future technology. Teachers will not need to have a real burning building to help trainees learn how to fight fires: they will be able to use virtual reality instead. Although not the real thing, this will be an invaluable training aid.

In the future, too, houses can carry their own fire detection systems. These are different from smoke detectors, which give warning of a fire, but do not say exactly where it is. The new detectors can be placed in the rooms of a house, and if a fire breaks out, they will tell firefighters exactly where it is.

FIRE SPY, THE ROBOT FIREFIGHTER

Firefighters face enormous dangers when they go to the scene of a fire: collapsing ceilings, fumes from poisonous chemicals, or the risk of getting trapped by the blaze they are trying to control. In the future, however, machines are going to take over in the shape of Fire Spy, the Robot Firefighter. Fire Spy can be controlled from a safe distance, more than 300 feet (91 m) away, and enters a building on

Left: New York City firefighters stand by as a column of fire shoots out of a broken underground gas pipe on Fifth Avenue.

fire to search for chemicals or other materials that are inflammable. Fire Spy will provide a safe way of removing these materials to places well away from the fire without firefighters having to risk their lives to do it.

The West Yorkshire Fire Service in Britain learned about the tremendous risks involved when they fought a fire at a chemical factory in the city of Bradford in 1992. One of the factory's warehouses contained 600 tons (540 metric tonnes) of the chemical acrylo-nitryl. Acrylo-nitryl is a powerful explosive, and the Fire Service believes that if it had blown up, large areas of the city of Bradford would have been destroyed.

Fortunately, the acrylo-nitryl did not explode, but another fire could bring the same danger. This is where Fire Spy will help. Fire Spy was designed to work in temperatures that human beings cannot survive—up to 1,500°F (816°C). The robot has a strong, grabbing arm in front and is equipped with infrared and ordinary cameras, which can send back pictures to a video screen. In this way, the firefighter controlling Fire Spy can see what is happening inside the burning building and where the flammable materials are.

FROM "BUCKET BRIGADES" TO BEYOND

It is not practical, of course, to think that all fires can be prevented, however much modern technology is used in the fight against them. Fire has always been a wild spirit with a will of its own and a terrifying ability to destroy and devastate wherever it goes. Indeed, in ancient times, fire was regarded as a god, for it had such a terrible, all-consuming power over human life.

In Austin, Texas, a firefighter from a hazardous materials unit is hosed down by a colleague in a decontamination area, following an emergency call to a vehicle containing dangerous chemicals.

Firefighting has come a long way since then, especially in the recent past. After all, only three centuries have passed since fires were being fought by the age-old method of bucket brigades—and not always successfully, either. Technology has produced better pumps or better water supplies, and these have played their part in improving firefighting methods, but it is high-tech that has made the biggest difference. For the first time in history, it has given firefighters and fire victims a real chance to get the better of fire. As this technology progresses, those chances are going to increase in the 21st century and beyond.

GLOSSARY

AMMS: Aerial Mobile Mapping System; a computer database containing information about fires

Arson: the crime of setting a building on fire deliberately

Breathing apparatus: a helmet and mask that enables firefighters to breathe when working in the smoke and fumes created by fire

Conflagration: large, disastrous fire

Firebreak: materials used to hinder a fire's progress

Fire extinguisher: equipment using water or chemicals for putting out fires

Fire hydrant: small but easy-to-see towers on the sidewalks of a city; firefighters attach their hoses to the hydrant so that they can use the city's water supply to fight the fire

Fire police: firefighters who are also police officers

Fire victim: person trapped or injured by a fire

Fuselage: the main body of an aircraft

Ground Zero: the site of the World Trade Center in New York City after its twin towers were destroyed by terrorists on September 11, 2001

Hotshots: wildland firefighters

Insulae: Roman apartment block

Lyre: stringed muscial instrument popular in the Middle Ages

Multiple dwelling: a building, usually three or four stories high, housing up to three families

Pall: a heavy fog or smoke causing the sky to be gloomy

Private dwelling: building housing one or two families

Rappelers: firefighters who slide down ropes from a helicopter (see *Smokejumpers*)

RAWS: Remote Automated Weather Station used for detecting signs of a fire in remote or faraway places

Sizing up: deciding what has to be done to rescue fire victims or fight a fire

Smokejumpers: firefighters who parachute from aircraft into a forest where there is a fire (see *Rappelers*)

VES: Vent—open windows to let heat and smoke out; Enter— rooms inside a blazing building; Search—for fire victims

Vigiles: people who stand guard at night

Wildfires: rapidly spreading fires that often occur in the wildlands

Wildlands: wide open spaces, forests, mountains, or other remote areas

CHRONOLOGY

ca. 4000 B.C.: The establishment of the first cities in Mesopotamia (Iraq) increases the risk of fire because so many people now live close together.

2nd century: Leather water pumps for firefighting are used in ancient Egypt.

A.D. **61**: Rebel queen Boudicca of the Iceni burns London, in the Roman province of Britannia.

A.D. **63**: Roman vigiles in London watch out for fires.

A.D. **64**: Great fire in ancient Rome; Emperor Nero is blamed for starting it.

A.D. **390**: Fire at Alexandria, Egypt destroys the 700,000 books of the city library.

A.D. **872**: King Alfred of Wessex (southern England) introduces the *curfew*. "Curfew" comes from the French *couvre-feu,* cover fire. People now had to put covers over their household fires at night to protect against the risk of fire.

1212: London Bridge burns down.

1648: Fire inspectors are appointed in New Amsterdam (New York) to make sure fire regulations are observed.

1650: First fire engine—a tub filled with water and having a pump for pouring water on fires.

1666: Great Fire of London, which destroyed most of the city.

1680: First fire brigade is established in London; first fire brigade established in Boston, Massachusetts.

1735: Benjamin Franklin organizes the first volunteer fire brigade in America.

1765: Future president George Washington brings the first fire engine to America from Britain.

1818: Molly Williams becomes the first woman firefighter in the United States.

1820: In York (now Toronto, Canada), every householder is ordered to keep two buckets for carrying water to fires.

1829: First steam-driven fire engine.

1870: Ladders are first used to fight fire in the higher stories of buildings.

1871: Great Chicago Fire.

1906: San Francisco earthquake and fire.

ca. 1918: First firefighting departments.

1919: Aircraft first used to fight fires in California.

1991: Two serious wildland fires in East Bay Hills area, California.

1994: Forest fire on Storm King Mountain, Colorado.

1994: Earthquake and fires in Los Angeles.

1998: Huge wildland fires in northern Florida and New Mexico.

2000: July 25, crash of Air France Concorde, Paris.

2000–2001: Serious fires in the forests of Alberta, Canada.

2001: September 11, the twin towers of the World Trade Center, New York City, collapse after two airplanes fly directly into them.

FURTHER INFORMATION

USEFUL WEB SITES

Fire disasters: forestry/about.com/library/weekly/aa052100.htm

Firefighting robots: easyweb.easynet.co.uk

Fire on the Mountain (South Canyon Fire, 1994): www.wildfire news.com/fireonthemountain/

Fire research: www.dbce.csiro.au/inno-web/0800/fire_research.htm

Florida Fires (2001): www.canoe.ca/CNEWSScienceNews/fire_may29-cp.html

Terrorist Attack, New York City, September 11, 2001: www. channel4.com/science/microsites/S/science/news_towers.html

FURTHER READING

Gorell, Gena K. *Catching Fire: The Story of Firefighting*. Toronto, Ontario: Tundra Books, 1999.

Norman, John. *Fire Officer's Handbook of Tactics*. New Jersey: Fire Engineering Books, Penny Well Publishing, 1998.

Pickett, George. *The Brave: A Story of New York City's Firefighters*. Fredericksburg, VA: Brick Tower Press, 2002.

Paul, Caroline. *Fighting Fire*. New York: St. Martin's Press, 1999.

Smith, D. *Firefighters: Their Lives in Their Own Words*. New York: Broadway Books, 2002.

ABOUT THE AUTHOR

Brenda Ralph Lewis is a prolific writer of books, articles, television documentary scripts, and other materials on history, royalty, military subjects, aviation, and philately. Her writing includes many books on ancient history, culture, and life; books on World War II: *The Hitler Youth: The* Hitlerjugend *in Peace and War 1933–1945* (2000), *Women At War* (2001), and *The Story of Anne Frank* (2001). She has also written or contributed to numerous books for children, including *The Aztecs* (1999), *Stamps! A Young Philatelist's Guide* (1998), and *Ritual Sacrifice: A History* (2002). She lives in Buckinghamshire, England.

INDEX

References in italics refer to illustrations

Aerial Mobile Mapping System
  (AMMS) 82–3
aircraft fires 66, 67, 69, 70
  airports 66, 68–73
  Concorde 71
  extinguishing 69, 70–3
  evacuation 71–2, 74–6
  investigations 76–7
  precautions 65–6
aircraft, wildland fires 56, 58–9, 62,
  80
airports, air crashes 66, 68–73
apartment buildings 39–40
arson 27–9, 46
aviation fuel 67, 70, 76

breathing apparatus 26, 27, 29
bucket brigades 16–17, 88–9
bushfires see wildland fires

Charles II, King of England 13
chemical fires 21, 74, 88, 89
cigarettes, fire cause 41, 42, 51
city fires
  apartment buildings 39–40
  causes 40–2
  eyewitness accounts 45, 46
  houses 42–6, 48
  reaching 37–9
  rescue 39–40, 43–6
  statistics 42, 48
Concorde 71
crowd control 31

database, fires 84

earthquakes 48
engines, fire see fire engines
Evelyn, John, diarist 15
explosions 21, 41, 86

fire brigades, first 15–17
fire deaths
  arson 46
  city fires 12, 18, 28,
  housing 48
  World Trade Center 24, 76–7
fire engines 13, 14, 26, 38
  city fires 37–9
  early 13, 17, 18
  foam pumpers 70–3
fire extinguishers 40, 65, 73
fire hydrants 8, 39

fire police 31
Fire Spy 87–8
fire towers 53–4
fireboats 68, 74
firefighting
  early history 9–12
  equipment 26–7, 29, 40, 47,
    79–81, 87–9
  new technology 21, 79–84, 87–9
  training 23–6, 28–32, 87
fires, ancient Rome 11–12
fires see also aircraft fires; city fires;
  house fires; New York; wildland
  fires
  apartment buildings 39–40
  arson 27–9, 46
  causes 40–2, 51, 53, 57
  chemical 21, 74, 88, 89
  Chicago 18, 21
  database 84
  detection 48, 53–4, 65
  Italy 41, 48, 49
  London 12–15
  railroad trains 68
  ships 68, 74
  sizing up 32–5
  spread 39, 77
  statistics 25, 30, 33, 42, 48, 57,
    72
  types 26–7
first aid 24
foam 69, 70–3, 79
foam pumpers 70–3
forest fires see wildland fires
Franklin, Benjamin 15–16

gas explosions 21, 41, 86
Great Chicago Fire 18, 21
Great Fire of London 12–15
Ground Zero see World Trade Center,
  New York

heat detectors 65, 79, 81, 82–3
helicopters 55, 56, 58–9
hotshots 59–63
house fires 25, 42–6, 48

ladders, escape 27, 29, 37, 39, 45
lightning 51, 53, 57
lightning rods 16

National Guard 56, 60
Nero, Emperor of Rome 10, 11–12
New York City 8, 27, 30, 72, 75,
  86
  World Trade Center 22, 24, 36,
  38, 64, 67, 73

parachutists see smokejumpers

poems 34–5

railroad train fires 68
rappeling 63
Report from Engine Company 82, 46
rescue
  aircraft fires 71–2, 74–7
  city fires 29, 39–40, 43–6
  training 23, 26–7
  wildland fires 54
  World Trade Center 22, 24
robots 81, 87–8
Roman Empire 9–11, 12

saving lives see rescue
Search and Rescue Task Force
  (SARTF) 54
September 11, 2001 22, 24, 36, 67,
  73, 76–7
  see also World Trade Center
ship fires 68, 74
sizing up, fires 32–5
smoke
  alarms 48, 65
  inhalation 43–6
smokejumpers 62–3

technology, firefighting 21, 79–84,
  87–9
thermal imaging cameras 73, 82–3,
  87
thunderstorms see lightning

vent, enter, search (VES) procedure
  45–6
vigiles 10–11, 12
volunteer firefighters 34

Washington, George 18, 19
wildland fires 26–8, 50, 78, 85
  aircraft 56, 58–9, 62, 80
  causes 51–3, 57
  containment 56–60, 81–2
  detection 53–4, 82–3
  helicopters 55, 56, 58–9
  hotshots 59–63
  rappelers 63
  smokejumpers 62–3
  spread 54–6, 59
  weather conditions 53, 54, 57
women firefighters 17, 20
World Trade Center, New York City
  22, 24, 36, 38, 64, 73
  cause of collapse 67, 76–7
World War II 20